Dear Parent:

Congratulations! Your child is taking the first steps on an exciting journey. The destination? Independent reading!

STEP INTO READING® will help your child get there. The program offers books at five levels that accompany children from their first attempts at reading to reading success. Each step includes fun stories, fiction and nonfiction, and colorful art. There are also Step into Reading Sticker Books, Step into Reading Math Readers, Step into Reading Write-In Readers, Step into Reading Phonics Readers, and Step into Reading Phonics First Steps! Boxed Sets—a complete literacy program with something to interest every child.

Learning to Read, Step by Step!

Ready to Read   Preschool–Kindergarten
• big type and easy words • rhyme and rhythm • picture clues
For children who know the alphabet and are eager to begin reading.

Reading with Help   Preschool–Grade 1
• basic vocabulary • short sentences • simple stories
For children who recognize familiar words and sound out new words with help.

Reading on Your Own   Grades 1–3
• engaging characters • easy-to-follow plots • popular topics
For children who are ready to read on their own.

Reading Paragraphs   Grades 2–3
• challenging vocabulary • short paragraphs • exciting stories
For newly independent readers who read simple sentences with confidence.

Ready for Chapters   Grades 2–4
• chapters • longer paragraphs • full-color art
For children who want to take the plunge into chapter books but still like colorful pictures.

STEP INTO READING® is designed to give every child a successful reading experience. The grade levels are only guides. Children can progress through the steps at their own speed, developing confidence in their reading, no matter what their grade.

Remember, a lifetime love of reading starts with a single step!

For my aunts, Nikki Corey
and Carol Klein, with love
—S.C.

With grateful acknowledgment to Patrick M. Leehey, Research Director of the Paul Revere House, for his time and expertise in reviewing this book.

Photo credit: Portrait of Paul Revere holding a piece of silverware © Bettmann/Corbis

www.stepintoreading.com

Educators and librarians, for a variety of teaching tools, visit us at www.randomhouse.com/teachers

Library of Congress Cataloging-in-Publication Data
Corey, Shana.
Paul Revere's ride / by Shana Corey ; illustrated by Chris O'Leary. — 1st ed.
   p.   cm. — (Step into reading. Step 3 book)
ISBN 0-375-82836-2 (trade) — ISBN 0-375-92836-7 (lib. bdg.)
1. Revere, Paul, 1735–1818—Juvenile literature.   2. Statesmen—Massachusetts—Biography—Juvenile literature.   3. Massachusetts—Biography—Juvenile literature.   4. Massachusetts—History—Revolution, 1775–1783—Juvenile literature.   [1. Revere, Paul, 1735–1818.
2. Silversmiths.   3. Massachusetts—History—Revolution, 1775–1783.]   I. O'Leary, Chris, ill.
II. Title.   III. Series: Step into reading. Step 3 book.
F69.R43 C67 2004 973.3'311'092—dc22 2003023611

Printed in the United States of America   First Edition   10 9 8 7 6 5 4 3 2 1

STEP INTO READING, RANDOM HOUSE, and the Random House colophon are registered trademarks of Random House, Inc.

STEP INTO READING®

STEP 3

PAUL REVERE'S RIDE

by Shana Corey

illustrated by Chris O'Leary

Random House 🏠 New York

Paul Revere was a busy man.

Every day, he worked

in his silver shop.

He made buckles and bowls.

He made teapots and trays.

He even made a chain

for someone's pet squirrel.

When people in Boston
needed a false tooth,
they came to Paul Revere.

That's because Paul

was also a dentist.

He made false teeth

out of hippo tusks!

At night,

Paul closed his shop.

He tucked his children into bed.

He kissed his wife goodbye.

Then he went to a secret club.

The club was called

the Sons of Liberty.

The Sons of Liberty were mad
because America was not
its own country.
America was a colony.
It was ruled by Great Britain.
British soldiers lived
in America.

The British added extra charges,
or taxes, on things
the American colonists bought.

Many colonists did not think

this was fair.

They did not have a vote

in making the laws.

So they did not want

to follow them.

When the tax collectors came,

the colonists tied them

to flagpoles.

They covered them
with tar and feathers.

They chased them out of town!

The British stopped
some of the taxes.
But not all of them.
They taxed tea.
In 1773,
three British ships
landed in Boston.
They were filled with tea!

Paul Revere and
the Sons of Liberty
decided to fight back!
They painted their faces
so no one would know
who they were.
Then they climbed
on board the ships.

Smash!

They opened

the chests of tea.

Splash!

They dumped

the tea into the water!

"That's it!"

said the King of England.

He sent more soldiers to Boston

to make the colonists behave.

The colonists called

the soldiers Redcoats

because of their red uniforms.

One day,

Paul heard that the Redcoats

were planning to march

on the town of Concord.

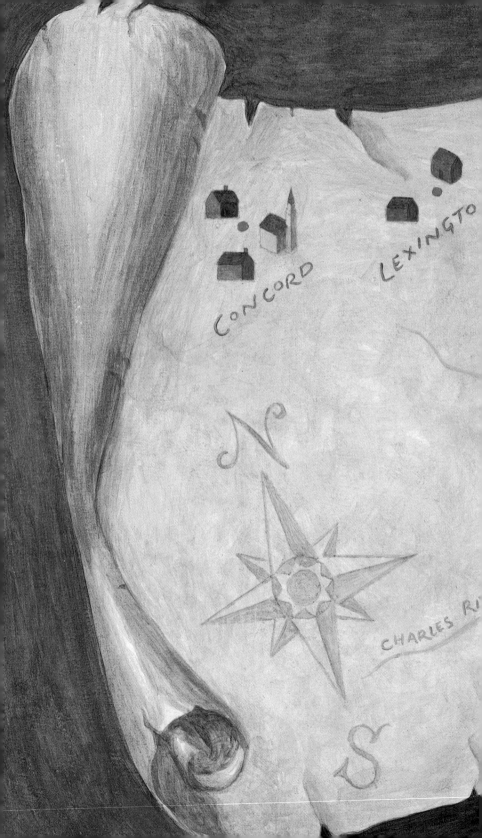

Concord was across the river
from Boston.
Two of the colonial leaders—
Sam Adams and John Hancock—
were staying nearby
in the town of Lexington.
If the Redcoats found them,
they would arrest Sam and John.
Paul had to warn them!

BOSTON

It was a risky job.

Paul and his friend Robert Newman

had a plan.

Robert would hang lanterns

in Christ Church.

They would be a warning

in case Paul did not make it.

One lantern meant

the Redcoats were going

to Concord by land.

Two lanterns meant

they were crossing

the river in boats,

then marching to Concord.

On April 18, 1775,

the Redcoats

boarded their boats.

Paul told Robert

to hang two lanterns.

The Redcoats were

going by water!

Paul raced to the river.
Two of his friends waited
with a rowboat.
There are many stories
about what happened next.

One story says that

Paul was in such a hurry

he forgot his spurs.

Luckily,

Paul's little dog

had followed him.

Paul scribbled a note.

He stuck it into the dog's collar.

"Take this home!"

said Paul.

The dog ran off.

A few minutes later,

he came back.

He had the spurs in his collar!

Another story says that
Paul climbed into the boat.
But he had forgotten
something else!
What if the Redcoats heard
the boat's oars creaking?
A neighbor lady
leaned out of her window.
"What's wrong?" she whispered.
Paul told her his problem.

The lady threw
her petticoat down.
"Good luck!" she said.
Paul tore the petticoat
into strips.
He tied them around the oars.

We do not know
if these stories are true.
But we do know
that Paul and his friends
made it past the British.
When they landed,
Paul borrowed a horse.
Then he galloped off
into the night.

Paul warned all the houses
he passed.
He had not gone far
when a Redcoat spotted him.
"Giddyup!" cried Paul.
He left the officer in the dust.

Paul finally found Sam Adams
and John Hancock.
He told them his news.
Then he headed to Concord.
Two other colonists
went with him.

Suddenly six Redcoats
jumped out of the woods.
The other riders escaped.
But Paul was surrounded.
Was this the end
for Paul Revere?

No!

Paul thought fast!

He told the Redcoats

that hundreds of colonists

were on their way!

The soldiers were scared.

They took Paul's horse.

Then they rushed off

to save themselves.

By now, it was almost morning.

Paul had been riding all night!

But he had one more job to do.

John Hancock had told Paul
there were important papers
in a trunk in the town tavern.
Paul had to get them—
before the Redcoats did!
He hurried to the tavern.
Paul and a friend
found the trunk.

But when they got outside,
the town square was filled
with Redcoats!

Bang!

Paul heard a shot!

Many people call it

"the shot heard 'round the world."

That's because it was

the first shot

of the American Revolution.

The war lasted for eight years.

Paul stopped making silver.

Instead, he made

cannons and gunpowder.

He printed money

for the colonists to use.

In 1783, the colonists
won the war!
America became
its own country.

Paul went back to making silver.
He was still a busy man.
He had lots of children
and *lots* of grandchildren.

In his spare time,

he opened a hardware store

and a copper mill.

He also learned

to make bells.

For years,
not many people knew
about Paul's ride.
Then in 1860,
a poet named
Henry Wadsworth Longfellow
wrote a poem about it.
Paul Revere became famous.

And he still is.

Today in Boston,

Christ Church still stands—

only now it is called

Old North Church.

Paul's silver still shines.

Paul's house still
welcomes visitors.

And Paul's bells
still ring out
for all to hear.

Paul Revere was born in December 1734. He died on May 10, 1818.

We know a lot about his ride because he wrote about it. But there are some things that we do not know. For instance, we think the horse he rode was named Brown Beauty. But we do not know for sure. We also do not know the name of Paul's dog. But we do know it was a small dog. We know this because Boston had a rule that no one could have a dog taller than 11 inches!